LILO SPEAKS:

A Memoir

—————❧—————

with Tom Adams

LILO SPEAKS: A MEMOIR

Copyright © 2011 Tom Adams

ISBN 978-0-9834370-0-0

Printed in China

Published by:

Big Hat Press
Lafayette, California
www.bighatpress.com

in conjunction with

Thomas Berryhill Press

Cover Image: Lilo Basch, 1939. Lilo was 20 years old and lived in Java after her escape from Nazi Germany.

Cover Design: Molly Williams

This memoir is based on a series of videotaped interviews conducted in 2010-2011 at Lilo's home in Mill Valley, California. Tom Adams, a San Francisco Bay Area author, conducted and edited the interviews. Adams prepared this manuscript for publication. Brandon Katcher, a resident of San Rafael, California, videotaped the interviews.

Additional assistance was provided by Phillip Adams, Rita Charles, Annie Graeber, Joseph Vanderliet, Anna and Richard Lininger, and the Oakwood Athletic Club where the concept for this memoir originated.

CONTENTS

INTRODUCTION

My mother, Liselotte (Lilo) Basch Heller, was born in 1921 in Liegnitz, Germany. Her parents, George and Johanna Basch, were German Jews. Germany was a troubled country, reeling from defeat in World War I. Proverty, rampant unemployment and a profound loss of German pride swept across the nation. The Basch's owned a thriving business and were considered middle class. For the most part, Lilo's childhood was happy. She loved school, hiking and riding her bicycle through the Riesengebirge Mountains. As the years passed, her world lost its beauty and innocence as darkness descended upon Germany.

The rise of Nazism, led by Adolf Hitler, stoked profound fears among German Jews. In his book, Mein Kampf, Hitler laid out his plan for the extermination of Jews and the ascendance of a master Aryan Race. On January 30, 1933, Adolf Hitler was appointed Chancellor of The Third Reich by the aging and reluctant President of the Republic, Field Marshall von Hindenburg. Hitler began to execute his plan. In 1935, with the passage of the Nuremburg Laws, Jews were forbidden from attending German public schools or serving in public or private professions.

Fearing for Lilo's safety, her parents sent her to the Buser Institute in Telufen Village, a private girl's school in Switzerland, that became a safe haven for wealthy European children. When the Nazis confiscated the Basch family business, they could no longer afford to keep Lilo in the Swiss school. In 1937, she returned to Germany to attend a Jewish girl's school in Breslau.

Conditions for the Jews deteriorated in the late 1930s. The Basch family began to arrange to buy passage out of

Germany, while it was still possible to do so. The Basch's decided to flee to Ecuador and Lilo sailed to Java.

This Memoir recounts the challenges Lilo faced and the skills she developed to resolve them. She survived the persecution of the Jews under the Nazis and escaped at age 17 on a luxury liner to Java in the Dutch East Indies. After the surprise attack on Pearl Harbor, the Japanese occupied Java on February 8, 1942. Lilo was arrested by the Japanese on October 3, 1943, and imprisoned. At the conclusion of World War II, in 1945, she remained in Java and worked as a nurse in Jakarta. From 1945 to 1946, she was caught in the violent Dutch Indonesian Civil War. Lilo escaped to Manila, in the Philippines, and finally relocated to San Francisco in late 1946.

There are few other young women who have encountered as many crises as she did and survived. Lilo provides insights into the capacity of one woman to endure, grow and remain true to her humane convictions. During her lifetime, she has generously helped those threatened by the more powerful. Lilo rarely spoke to her children of these painful atrocities. I knew only bits and pieces of her turbulent past. The single most important quality that I recognize is her total commitment to help the oppressed and those in need. On many occasions, she took up varied causes, donated money and fought for them. Today, after all these years, my mother feels comfortable enough to recount these stories.

When my mother settled in San Francisco, in 1946, she took up unpopular causes. Her work with radical labor union members was noted by the F.B.I. in the early 1950s. She and my father worked with left wing groups and supported many Socialist and Communist causes. They operated, pro bono, the Progressive Book Store on Valencia Street. The store served as a repository of radical literature, as well as a meeting place and refuge for many of San Francisco's radicals. In 1984, Lilo returned to East Germany, for the first time in 45 years, to serve as a delegate to the International Women's Peace Congress. Lilo is a pacifist.

Today, in 2011, Lilo lives alone in Mill Valley, in Marin County, California where she is surrounded by her extended family. At 89 years of age, she continues to support causes that touch her heart and stoke her determination to fight oppression, inequality and discrimination against women and all minorities. At the front of her home, a sign pleads, "Bring the Troops Home!"

Michael Heller

PREFACE

March 9, 2010

Troubled sleep. Nightmares! Oh, yes! Those came that very night just as I had expected when I had agreed to tell my stories; stories I had not shared with my family. I had always said, "It's too painful and no one cares any more. Why dredge up the past? No!" But, reluctantly I had agreed to let others know. A few things remain too painful to relate, but, I am speaking now.

I don't forget the Japanese prison camps; the bedbugs, the rats. And you don't forget the sewer overflowing. When it did, we screamed bloody murder. The stench was terrible. Most of us got sick. Many died. I don't forget the brutality, the pain and fear at the hands of the Japanese.

One afternoon I sat at the kitchen table to look through the family albums; tattered and worn, yet the only remaining visual history. No one else is alive to tell our story. The photos must suffice to stir my memory. My parents had brought the albums from Germany in 1939, when they escaped to Quito, Ecuador. The photos are faded. Many in sepia hue, browned even more by time and transport over the last 82 years. Each one evokes memories; some happy, but mostly sad and foreboding. Here is my grandmother Basch, firm but gentle, murdered in 1943 at age 75 in or on her way to Buchenwald. Two versions have been told. First, one says she died of a heart attack while herded onto a crowded cattle train used by the Nazis to transport human cargo to their death camps. The second version is that she was exterminated in the camp's ovens. What's the difference? Either one is murder.

I looked quickly at the photos of my nieces, nephews and cousins. I can't dwell on their faces for too long. Too painful. These young people, so filled with promise and innocence; their lives snuffed out because they were Jews. No one was given the opportunity to leave a legacy for our family. Some might have been physicians, others in business, others teachers or maybe even a poet or an artist. They should have been allowed to enrich our family's heritage, to live a full life; but madness and mayhem prevailed. I hope Germans realize the steep price they have paid for eliminating the talents and humanity of so many.

I see the picture of a favorite uncle, sitting in his armchair, smiling and content. Often, I rode my bike to visit him in Liegnitz, to a home filled with love and encouragement. We would talk for hours and then he's gone! Anger!

The older man in the white suit is Mr. Jacobson, an executive with the Palmolive company in the Dutch East Indies. The Japanese occupiers of the Indies threw him in a prison camp in 1942, where he died of pneumonia two years later.

The picture of my schoolmates reminds me of happier days. I am the one with glasses in the front row. Next to me is a brave little German girl leaning against a German Jew. She was brave! Soon all of that would change. I have lost so many of my family and friends to the horrors of Nazi tyranny.

By 1945 all of our Basch family who remained in Germany, except for a few who had collaborated with the Nazis, were murdered. A few, who did heed the impending warning signs of doom, fled to safety in other lands. My parents and I did escape.

As I look through these albums, my heart sinks.

I cry silently with anger. The enormity of this tragedy is overwhelming.

When the barbarous Nazis sought their final solution, our entire family witnessed and experienced the destruction so totally planned by Hitler in 1924 and executed by his legions with adoring support from most Germans. I, alone at age 89, live to record these tragic and turbulent years. Sadly, my story is only one of many that must be told by other Jewish families. A full accounting of the holocaust is demanded!

Sixty five years ago, in 1945, Germany and Japan surrendered and World War II ended. Its history has not. Germany, Italy, Japan and their other collaborators attacked many countries. They murdered or enslaved the native people, took their land, resources and tried to rob them of their national pride. They were ruthless. They almost won; instead they were left in ruins. Most wars do end that way, but, in the process, the world suffered untold damage.

Our stories must be heard and remembered. Today I continue to long for peace in this troubled world.

Lilo Basch Heller

George and Johanna Basch, married on March 15, 1918.

Johanna Basch, Lilo's mother, 1939, prior to the escape to Ecuador. The photograph is an official visa passport with the green Nazi stamp of approval. The Star of David stamp appears in green near her collar.

George Basch, Lilo's father, 1939, prior to the escape to Ecuador in an official Nazi visa photo.

Martha Basch, the stepmother of George Basch

George Basch, 1934, at a spa in Czechoslovakia.

Sophie Basch, Lilo's grandmother, died in
Buchenwald at age 75.

Lilo Basch, 1931, age 10

Map of Germany showing Silesia in 1919.

CHAPTER I

A Jewish Girl in Nazi Germany

❦

They fell in love when they were fourteen. They were first cousins. Their fathers were brothers. The Basch family from Liegnitz, Germany visited the Basch family in Rostock on the Baltic Coast during summers. George Basch married Johanna Basch in Rostock a few years later. Such a marriage would be frowned upon today, but at the turn of the century, nothing was said. They settled in Liegnitz. They had government health insurance which was provided by Otto Bismarck, the Kaiser. Our family had a stable income. I even had a nursemaid.

My grandmother embroidered the German national flag. It rests in a museum in Liegnitz. I saw it several times as a child. My grandmother died of a heart attack in 1898. She had three sons. My Uncle Martin was five years older than my Uncle Hans, who served in the Navy. My father, George, was the youngest.

My father was born in Berlin in 1886. His family moved to Liegnitz where he went into business with his father. At first, they cured leather for gloves in a town creek ten miles from Liegnitz. Later, they switched to selling casings for local butchers who made their own sausage. They bought wholesale imported casings. They cleaned the casings for many butchers in Silesia, in the region where I grew up. Everyone knew my father because he grew up in Liegnitz. He traveled to various towns, some in Czechoslovakia, where he bought me a pair of leather gloves. My mother kept the books for the company. After my grandfather died, when I was one year old, she ran the business quite well.

When World War I started, my father refused to enlist. The family were pacifists. He intentionally broke his trigger finger so the Army wouldn't take him. It took a long time for the finger to heal, but he didn't have to fight. Toward the end of the war, he was sent to Poland to serve guard duty, but he never had to fight. His parents instilled in him the will not to fight. They were strongly against World War I.

I was born in July 1921, and remained an only child. I was named Liselotte Basch. Everyone called me Lilo. We lived in a house that was heated by a pot belly stove in each room. The stoves were made of different colored tile. The maid cleaned them, and then made a fire with coals so we would stay warm at night. You bought the coal in July to last through the cold winters. Liegnitz is situated at the foot of mountains and is known for its cold winters.

When I was born, I had a defect in my left eye and was forced to wear glasses early on. I had what they call a lazy eye, which required that I do many eye exercises. I managed. Lucky me! Doctors operated on my eye when I was two, but I lost vision in my left eye later. I stood out in schools since I was the only girl wearing glasses. I went to the first grade in public school in 1927. I remember my nursemaid took me to school and picked me up. School was fun. We went to the school from ten to two and in the winter from eight to one. There were about fifty kids in the class. You had to get up when the teacher came in and then she told you to sit down. If you had something to say, you raised your hand and she would call on you and you would talk standing up. When she told you sit down, you sat down, you behaved. So it was very strict. When kids talked in class, she called them to the front of class where she slapped their hand. I never got my hand slapped but I got into other trouble there. The school was near a park. They called it a garden school even though we didn't have any flowers. We wore aprons over our dresses. In the fourth grade I got the mumps. My mother took me to the Baltic Sea to recover. I had lots of colds during my early school years.

There was a lot of prejudice taught in school – even before Hitler. One teacher talked about those dirty people in Estonia and Poland. I put my hand up and said they look like us. She said we had to bring money to school to help support our German schools in the colonies in Africa and Latin America. They didn't want the Germans to learn those dirty languages so they built their own schools. I thought that was racist so I wouldn't buy stamps to support those schools. I thought the German kids should learn the languages of the countries they occupied.

The principal called my mother to the school. The principal told my mother that I must be like the other children. My mother said she would try to change my attitude. It didn't work.

My Early Interest in Politics

People were very conscious of politics. I knew Hitler started his Nazi party in a cellar in Munich and more and more people joined. In 1929, Chancellor Hindenburg came to Liegnitz and rode around in an open car to greet the townspeople. Hindenburg was a famous General in the Kaiser's Army in World War I. All our neighbors wanted to welcome him. He was known for some big victories, including the defeat of the Russians in East Prussia. Some townspeople decided to fly the old Kaiser's flag to welcome him. I wanted to put up a flag, but not the Kaiser's. I had a German Republic flag, the same one they use today. My father said, "No, that's dangerous." I refused to fly the Kaiser's flag. I got a good beating, but we settled on a flag of our area. That was my first introduction into politics. I was nine years old.

Across the street from our school was a big building occupied by the Socialist Party. It was customary to put your party's newspaper in a glass case outside. I could read and wanted to know what was in the paper. I was in third grade, so I read it. On the way to school was another building for the Communist Party. Well, I had to know what they had to say and I read their paper. Then I asked my parents all about it. They explained the two groups that were fighting each other for power.

When I got whooping cough, my mother took me to the mountains to recover. They found out I needed my tonsils out. I remember walking home with my mother and it didn't hurt. Later it hurt when I had ice cream. Finally, I could go back to school! One day I went to see my grandmother and I heard lots of yelling. There was a street demonstration. The Nazis were on one side and the Communists were on the other. When they met, they beat each other up. I had to see it, so I looked from my grandmother's balcony. That was my second introduction to politics. I'm still of the opinion that Hitler was very much liked by the Germans. He said, "I will bring you peace. Everybody will have jobs. That's what I bring you!" Well, it worked on the Germans. He got ninety eight percent of the votes in 1933 and was appointed Chancellor of the Third Reich by General Hindenburg.

My Education Was More than School Work

Our family liked to travel. I learned many things outside of school. We went on vacations to spas and to the Baltic Coast in the summers to visit relatives. I went with my father to see The Reichstag before it was burned by the Nazis in 1936. On one Easter vacation, we went by train to Dresden where we visited the beautiful museums.

I got my father to take me to the Museum of Hygiene where they had a human body made of glass. I looked at it for an hour. In Dresden we went to the Opera House and the museums and saw beautiful paintings. The porcelain was beautiful. Unfortunately, much of it was burned in the Allied bombings, on February 13, 1945. The local people had hidden much of the glass, porcelain and art works in the cellars in the calcium mines nearby.

My father and I liked to hike. Once I went with some friends into the nearby mountains. We climbed up the highest peak and stayed all night in a meadow. We had run out of money. We found a patch of wild blueberries and strawberries. We ate until we couldn't eat any more. We found a hay loft to sleep in. A German woman took us to a bakery to get some rolls. We went home the next day.

In 1936, my father took me to a museum where we spent a week looking at paintings. There was a special room with benches where you could sit to view a sixteenth century painting of the Madonna. The longer we sat, the more we saw the angels. That painting was taken to Leningrad by the Russians after the war and placed in the Hermitage Museum. Later they gave it back to the Germans. My favorite artist is Vincent van Gogh.

One time my father took me to a museum in Berlin. We were not allowed entry because we were Jews. I have never forgotten that cruelty. We were devastated.

One summer, in 1933, we went to Czechoslovakia to the spa. They had a big fountain and a little pond. You could rent boats in the summer and ice skate in the winter. Once we went ice skating. The little towns nearby had cobblestone streets. Some of the buildings date back to the eleventh century. There were many wars over the years between Poland and Germany. Frederick the Great got the town back for the Germans. We drove through the mountains to see castles along the rivers. Some towns had walls built around them.

We Helped Other Jews Escape

In 1933, my mother and I went to the mountains near the Czech border. My mother didn't like to walk, but I loved to hike. I walked up the mountains where I found a stone post. On one side it was marked "CS" for Czechoslovakia and on the other side "D" for Deutschland. I told my mother of this discovery. I found a way to cross Germany into Czechoslovakia without being seen!

One day, several days later, my mother and I were having coffee and cakes at a hotel near the bus station. We saw a couple with suitcases get off a bus. They were well dressed, but anxious looking. My mother knew right away that they

6

were planning to escape from Germany. We went to the couple and my mother said, "Give me the suitcases and go with my daughter. She will show you the way to Czechoslovakia. I will take your suitcases inside the border. Meet me there." She went to the Czech border and gave the guard a little money. She said her friends were meeting her. In the meantime, the couple and I walked up the trail to the stone post and down to the Czech side. They had escaped! The couple took their suitcases and disappeared after thanking my mother and me. The man was a Judge Advocate in Silesia. We felt proud!

The next year I was with another girl, a friend of my family. When we saw some frightened young people with suitcases, I said we had to help them. I'll show them how to escape. Sure enough they wanted to go with me up the mountain, over the hill and down into Czechoslovakia. They were free! I remember those desperate times very well.

I Was Taught the Classics

My mother was very well read. We had a big library at home. My mother was a secretary at Hinnsoff Publishers, that survived even the war and the breakup of Germany. The books were published in the Mecklenburg dialect. Lots of books surrounded me. I remember the Thomas Mann books, The Magic Mountain and Budden Bruck. I loved them. My father read the classics of Goethe and Schiller. Many of Mann's books were burned in Berlin when some students at the University of Berlin tossed them into a pile of burning books when the brown shirts began their rampage against Jewish intellectuals. I like most of German literature but not some of its music. Wagner was like a Nazi and so was

Richard Strauss. They hated the Jews. Hitler was inspired by Wagner's love of powerful gods and his heroic mysticism. In 1936, when Wagner's opera, the Niebelungen Ring, was performed in our town, our family did not go. Those four operas gave Hitler the myth of German superiority and the concept of a master race that was pitted against Jews. Wagner was convinced that the Jews were out to dominate the world with their money.

I was surrounded by art, music and books. On a trip to the nearby mountains, my father and I found the cabin where Mendelssohn wrote his tonal piece, Music without Words. There was a big plaque on the wall of the cabin. The plaque honored his cabin. Playing Mendelssohn's music was banned in Germany as well as the works of other Jewish composers. I am sure the Nazis took the plaque down because he was a Jewish composer. Hitler wouldn't give the Jews credit for anything they contributed to Germany. Hitler refused to acknowledge the contributions of anyone who was not Aryan except the Imperial Japanese.

When I was very young, I sat at the piano to listen to my mother and grandmother play. They were very accomplished. I'd ask to hear pieces by Beethoven and Mozart, my favorites. Although I could not play the piano myself, I could tell when a mistake was made. Those memories remain with me to this day. Why was all that culture and beauty taken away? I guess you will have to ask Hitler.

Our Jewish Faith

The Basch's were Jews. We didn't go by the dietary laws or other rituals. My father went to the synagogue in our hometown. On holidays, sometimes, he would drag my mother along. She wasn't much on religion and neither were her folks. When I got older, he dragged me to the synagogue. Although I was a girl, I got to sit next to him. He got permission. Women had to sit upstairs and men sat downstairs, but I was allowed to sit with my father. I went to a religious school once a week. We learned Jewish history. I learned what happened to the Jews in Palestine in the First Temple and the Second Temple. Many Jews went to Spain and became famous philosophers up until the twelfth century. Many went to the Netherlands. Others went to America, where a number of families who had lived in Spain, settled in New York.

My father went to the United States for a meeting. He was very active in a Jewish organization called B'nai Brith. He went to New York and then to a meeting in Washington, D.C. He spoke some English. He met with his oldest brother, Martin, who lived near New York City, in Pennsylvania. His brother warned him that fascism may come to the United States. My uncle said he didn't want our family to come to the United States and give his family trouble. He had told everybody he was Lutheran. He was an engineer at an American factory located in Eastern Pennsylvania. He made pretty good money. He had a wife and son, who later became an engineer and lived in New Jersey. My uncle had met his wife on the boat coming over from Germany. My father never went to the city where his brother lived. He did meet Uncle Martin again in New York. My dad had arranged for a train ride to Niagara Falls.

Our family missed a big chance to escape in 1935 to America, but my Uncle Martin was against it so we remained in Germany and experienced the Nazis. All of that could have been avoided if my uncle had not been so selfish and my father so weak.

Dark Clouds Gather

On January 31, 1933, I was in the fifth grade. Another girl and I had sleds which we used to visit our friends. When we stopped at a house, a man came out and said, "Hitler was appointed chancellor by Hindenburg." I took off for home on my sled. That's when and how I learned that our lives would change. Dark clouds began to gather.

By the time I was in the eighth grade, the 1935 Nuremburg Laws were enforced. School got worse and worse. People were very conscious of the changes. Many Jews began to plan their escape from Germany. Some families did go to South America. I learned a lot of geography by studying the maps of places we could safely go. I remember the capital of Honduras, Tegucigalpa. I loved saying that name over and over. We had bought a new radio in 1930. I never listened to Hitler nor did I see him speak. I did hear President Roosevelt's address to the German people. We were encouraged but nothing good happened.

Things got very bad by 1938. My father was arrested and was in jail for one night. I went on my bike to the train station where the Nazis were loading the prisoners on cattle cars to take them to Buchenwald. I stood on the fourth floor and watched as they called out the men's names. They didn't call my father's name. When the train left, he was returned to the jail. The Gestapo called my mother and told her to come for him at 2 o'clock the next day. When she arrived at the jail, she was told he had already gone home. She rushed home and embraced him. That is when my parents made the decision to escape.

I don't know for sure who pulled the strings to save my father. We think it was a German man whom my father had helped start a business a few years earlier. We had heard that he wrote a letter to his brother who was a big shot in the Nazi SS. He wrote, "Do something for George. He helped me with my business. I owe him something." We think he was the one who pulled the strings.

Uncle Alfred, a physician who lived in Breslau, died
in Buchenwald.

Fourth grade class picture, 1930, at the Green School in Liegnitz. Lilo is seated fourth from the right, in the front row. She wears long braids.

Ninth grade class picture, 1935. Lilo is the second student from the right, seated in the front row.

Liegnitz High School, 1932

CHAPTER II

Life in a Swiss Girl's School

In the evenings, in 1936, my parents and I poured over school catalogs, trying to decide which one I should attend outside of Germany. We settled on the Buser Institute in Telufen, Switzerland. The school was popular with young girls of means and attracted them from all over the world – Italy, Scotland, Wales, France, Holland, South America, the Dutch East Indies and others. We took the train to Switzerland, in 1936, to enroll me at Buser. The main building was on a hill surrounded with trees. I was assigned to a dormitory near the main building from which I could easily walk to classes.

My parents and I arrived on a Sunday. Everything was closed. We stayed overnight in a local hotel before going to the Institute for our orientation. The education at Buser was very advanced and students were expected to apply themselves seriously. We took classes in music, literature, science, history and art appreciation. I eagerly took to those courses.

Each table in the dining room was given a different foreign language which we learned to converse in with our classmates. Our table was assigned French. To graduate, you must learn the three languages of Switzerland – Italian, German and French.

I loved to hike, so I went down to the little town square. One day I saw the men voting; women weren't allowed to vote. The men voted by raising their hands, like in the first democracy in Greece. The Institute had a large swimming pool which I used when I had the time. Each morning all the girls gathered outside to do their physical exercises. We were a healthy and happy bunch. There were many trains in the area. I rode them up into the mountains and all over, exploring the beautiful countryside. I met Topsy, my best friend there. She was a vivacious girl from Java in the Dutch East Indies. She was mixed, Indonesian and Dutch. Later she would save my life.

Things were getting very bad for Jews in Germany in 1936. When I went home for Easter vacation in 1937, the Austrians would not let us travel by train through their country. We had to take the ferry across a big lake to leave Switzerland. When I returned to Liegnitz, all my Jewish friends had gone to a special Jewish school in Breslau, because the Nuremburg Laws excluded all Jews from public schools. Soon after I returned to the Buser Institute in 1937, the Nazis confiscated my father's business. They took away his financial livelihood. He could no longer afford to keep me at The Buser Institute after my second year. If I had been able to return, I would have been assigned to the Italian table. One of my roommates was Carla Berlusconi, a relative of today's Italian premier, Sylvio Berlusconi. She and I discussed politics. We did not approve of Benito Mussolini, Il

Duce. Fortunately, we were not taught the Nazi propaganda at Buser. I was forced to return to Germany at the end of my second year. I had completed the tenth grade.

When I returned to Germany, my parents arranged for me to attend the Jewish boarding school in Breslau, located in Silesia, where I had several relatives. In our classes we learned to crochet, knit and sew. I didn't like that very much. I had an older girlfriend, Terry, who helped me. The teachers knew I didn't do my own work. When I was assigned to knit socks, I had my grandmother do it.

We learned how to cook, organize a family budget and make good use of our time. I don't remember much of it. But I do remember that my relatives, Uncle Paul and the others who lived in Breslau, died in Buchenwald. That was their end.

After Stalin gave Silesia to the Poles, they renamed the town Wroclaw. I never wanted to see it again. There are too many bad memories.

Buser Institute, 1936, in Telufen, Switzerland. Lilo
attended this school for two years, 1936-1937.

Lilo at age 15 during summer vacation from the
Buser Institute, 1936. Lilo's braids were cut when
she enrolled in the Swiss girl's school.

Topsy Pantekoek, in the mountains located near
the Buser Institute.

CHAPTER III

Escape from the Nazis to Java in 1939

I came from my school in Switzerland to live in Germany for two more years. When you pull a string, the noose is wound tighter and tighter. That's what Hitler was doing to the Jews. In school, you didn't hear anything about politics, but I made it my business to learn. Although I was not religious, my parents arranged for me to see the Rabbi once a month to learn about the Jewish community. He brought me a paper, the national paper of Basel. Although I felt Switzerland was very conservative, that paper wasn't. In the winter of 1936, I read about the Spanish Civil War and the members of the International Abraham Lincoln Brigade, who were fighting against Franco and the Fascists. Those Spanish Loyalists were very brave, but they lost the Civil War to the Fascists who were sponsored by big business, Hitler and Mussolini. I read that Italy had invaded Ethiopia and had become a dangerous Fascist state. Carla Berlusconi told us about the Fascist marches that Italians were required to attend in Milano.

As I said earlier, my best girlfriend was Topsy Pante-koek, whose father was Dutch and her mother was mixed race. Topsy's complexion was not real white; she had dark eyes and dark hair. In 1938, I wrote a letter to Topsy. It was a desperate letter. I wrote that the Nazis were going to kill me if I did not escape from Germany. The situation in Germany was dire in 1938. In November, a very stupid Polish Jewish boy went to the German Embassy in Paris to kill the German Ambassador to France. Instead, he killed an aide to the Ambassador. As a consequence, the Polish Jews living in Germany were arrested, put on trains, and taken to a no-mans land on the other side of the Oder River. The Nazi trains came through Breslau. The Jews were there left to rot. Some of the German Jews brought clothing and food to them. I had neither to give. I thought this was a terrible thing to do to people. I think it was on November 1st and 2nd, 1938.

On November 8th, the Nazis burned synagogues throughout Germany. The destruction planned by the Nazi's was called, Kristallnacht or "the night of broken glass". Jewish shop windows were smashed and swastikas were painted on buildings. I rode my bike to downtown Breslau to see the damage. I was very frightened. After I saw the destruction, I rode my bike to a relative's house. They had just returned from a trip to Holland. My cousins, Sophie, Paul, Alfred and his wife, were sitting in Sophie's apartment. I screamed at them. "You must get out! The Nazis will kill you! How dare you stay!" They were not convinced. They stayed. Later, they and other Jews were rounded up and taken to Buchenwald, the concentration camp, where many were brutally exterminated.

My parents began to plan their escape from Germany.

My father dragged me to the Consulate of Ecuador in Berlin. They planned to take refuge in Ecuador. They paid for our visas in dollars. I said I did not want to go to Latin America because women could not work there. I told my father that I had written to Topsy to ask her to help me escape to Java. My dad said she would never be able to send me an affidavit to leave Germany. I said, "Yes, she will." I was so sure. I told my father that I'm not going to eat out of your pocket any more, because you have to go to work to take care of yourself and my mother. That was enough burden to put on you. "So, I'm not going to Ecuador," I told him. I got the visa for Java toward the end of December 1938.

Our Farewell

I stood in the train station with my parents, waiting for the Amsterdam train. I hugged my mother. I kissed my father. We cried, because we didn't know if or when we would see each other again. That farewell was the last time I saw my father. Eight years later I would reunite with my mother in Ecuador.

There were two ways to get to Holland. The northern route, the customary one, was difficult. The Nazis would frisk you and give you trouble. So, I took the southern route. I was alone and didn't want any trouble. They did ask to see my train ticket. When I arrived in Amsterdam, I took a cab to my relative's house. I had taught myself some Dutch. Nora Jacobson's relatives lived nearby. Nora and I would travel to Java together on a liner. Mr. Jacobson had made all the preparations for our trip. When I saw my relatives, I begged them to leave Holland. They said nothing is going to happen to us. Later the Nazis killed all of them after they invaded Holland in May 1940. That hurts me very much.

We had lunch on Sunday. On the next day we walked around Amsterdam. I was disappointed because I didn't get to see the museums. I met Nora at the harbor where we boarded the liner. I had a cabin to myself, a nice one with an outside window. Nora's was next to mine.

Our first stop was in Britain. It was rainy; it was misty. I was told the English don't have much sunshine. There is fog most of the time. I went to the post office and bought a postcard of the boat. That crazy money they had was quite different, a penny, whatever. I gave them a piece of paper and got change, which I saved for a keepsake. After lunch the boat left and we went through the Gulf of Biscayne. I remember we went through a real storm. I bought suppositories so I wouldn't get sick. Two days later we saw Gibraltar from the boat. I took some pictures.

The next stop was the city of Algiers. We went on a bus ride all around the city. We went into a mosque. Nobody said take your shoes off. Anyway we two crazy girls looked around and then went back to the boat. The boat next to us was a freighter. Two dark men started to talk to us. We went to the other side of the boat and didn't bother with those men.

The next stop was Genoa, in Italy. We went sightseeing. I don't know how long we walked, but I am sure we did not walk all the way to the town. When we came back, we couldn't find our boat. We were speaking German to each other. A man stopped, clearly an Italian man with an accent. "Where do you want to go?" he asked. He was a nice looking man, well dressed. He explained to us where the boat was. We were very surprised that he spoke German that well. He was probably a secret agent, but we didn't ask.

The boat left in the morning for Monte Carlo. I don't gamble. I think that's crazy. We watched them play roulette. The town has very pretty gardens and colorful buildings. Later we walked back to the boat. The gambling, I thought, is very sad, all those people sitting there throwing their money away. We sailed down the Italian coast and passed Stromboli, our first volcano. That afternoon we went through the Strait of Messina. I saw Mt. Etna from the boat. I knew what I was looking at because I had seen many pictures of the boat trips and vacations my family had taken to Italy.

We docked, port side, at four o'clock in the morning and were told that if we wanted to see something or buy something, we could go to town. It was very hot in May. We went out, walked around and dared to go one street down, and then back toward the boat. Two men were chasing us. We walked fast back to the boat. We were not going to get kidnapped. We saw children diving for coins so we threw some in the water. The police said, "Don't do that." The boat sailed and for the first time I saw a desert, a sand desert. Sand, sand, sand.

We went through the Suez Canal. It was extremely hot in the Gulf of Aden. The boat didn't stop because it was too hot. We sailed back to the ocean where it was kind of windy. We docked at Ceylon. It's now called Sri Lanka. We looked around. God, the poverty was terrible. We went on a tour to a Buddhist temple. We were invited by the Governor to have tea at his mansion. Mr. Jacobson had developed many contacts with important people in Asia through his leadership in the Palmolive Company in Java. His father had developed the process to make soap from dried copra. Those contacts allowed us to be welcomed in important places. We returned to the boat. We met a native teacher who talked to us about her country. We became quite friendly on the way to Singapore. The teacher was dark with black hair. The next stop was Sumatra. The capital of Sumatra was Medan. We took a cab from the harbor to the city to meet a lawyer. We had a very nice lunch at his house. There were many trees. I don't know what the trees were, maybe rubber. My father, who was a financial advisor to his B'nai Brith chapter in Liegnitz, and the lawyer were friends in Germany.

We went back to the boat and our next stop was Singapore, the destination of our new teacher friend. She was met by her sister and we walked to the hotel. We saw a sign that read "No dogs or Natives allowed". Oh, God. I wouldn't go in. It was too racist for me. We went to the teacher's house and met her two kids. The house was very poor, very sparsely furnished. The next morning they took us to the zoo. We went too close to a cage and the monkey grabbed the teacher's glasses. I was a scaredy cat. I wouldn't go near the cage. We went to a little airport where we had ice cream and coffee. For the first time, I watched a tennis match. Later they took us back to the boat.

My Arrival in Java

As we approached Jakarta, our liner was shot at by members of the Indonesian Freedom Movement. Sukarno was the head of the Indonesian Nationalists Party, which was fighting to overthrow the Dutch Colonial Authority. The freighter had stopped at Surabaja to pick up copra; dried coconut meat. I remember the night when they loaded it, and the next morning we left for Malacca. Next stop was Jakarta. It was called Batavia then. We were met by Nora's father. We drove to her house, which was located in Bangor. We were taken to the Governor's mansion, which was in the middle of a beautiful park. The trip from Germany lasted from May 3rd to June 1st. That trip to Java, and my two years at the boarding school in Switzerland, were among my happiest times. I was a typical German tourist.

Topsy had remained in Switzerland completing her education at the Buser Institute. Topsy's parents met me at the harbor. They had asked the Jacobson family to arrange for my travel to Java. Upon arrival, they took me to the Jacobson home, situated above a mountain plantation. We went to see Topsy's parents. We met her brother, a little boy about two years old who had a nursemaid. I never saw Topsy after I left the Swiss girl's school in 1937. I do not know what happened to her. I didn't worry because Topsy knew how to take care of herself. By then I was very tired and I slept mostly for five days. I guess the trip and the humidity got to me. Topsy's parents showed me how tea was dried. After a number of days, they drove me to Nora's house. They looked for a training program where I could learn skills to become self-sufficient.

My first job didn't work out. I was sent to a big home in Jakarta to be a companion to an elderly German Jewish lady. I had my own room. In September 1939, her husband came home. He praised Hitler. She was wealthy and much older than her husband. I am sure that is why he married her. When I found out that he was a Nazi, I packed my bags and rode my bicycle to my friend Nora's house nearby. I said, "I am not going back to be with those Nazis."

After that bad experience, I lived with a Jewish family. They had two young girls. They survived the war. As a matter of fact, we were together in the last prison camp. In a week they sent me to live with another family who lived in a big house. They said I was to train to be an x-ray technician at Princess Juliana Hospital. Luckily, it didn't work out. Then I began training to be a midwife. I began to work in a Lutheran hospital, where I worked from October 1939 to October 1941.

Indonesia was very different from Germany. With 96 active volcanoes, you had to be alert. When one threw off white smoke, you were safe. But when the smoke became dark, the volcano would erupt. Fortunately, I was spared that experience. I was told that two years before I had arrived, two days of ash covered Java. One volcano, Mt. Tijirama, was near the hospital where I worked. The mountain rose between two sugar factories, the one in Bandung and the one in Cheribon. Most of our patients were Indonesians who worked in those factories.

On my days off, I would ride my bike in the mountains near the hospital and along the large teak tree forests. Fifi, my dog, always accompanied me. A dog protected you against snakes. The cobra was the most poisonous snake in Java. One day when I came home from work, Fifi was at the door growling. She had spotted a cobra, coiled beneath a flower pot on my porch. She saved me from the snake. Everyone needed a dog.

I found a duplex near a sugar estate. It had two little rooms, one with a couch, bookcase and two windows. The other room had a table, a bed with a big mosquito net over it and a desk with two windows. The tables with exposed wooden legs couldn't stand on the cement floor because the ants would have had a field day eating them. The legs were placed in a metal bowl with water and petroleum that kept the ants away. The furniture was made of strengthened straw. My new house was near the hospital where I began my training to be a midwife.

The Lutheran hospital was run by a Dutch doctor and a mostly Indonesian staff. I was accepted by them. As a matter of fact, when the Dutch staff had a holiday, I would be responsible for taking care of the patients. It was a very good arrangement. By then, I only spoke Dutch and Indonesian.

On May 10, 1940, the Germans invaded Holland. The Dutch in Java didn't waste any time. They immediately picked up all Germans in the Dutch Indies except the German Jewish refugees. The Dutch were prepared. It went off like clockwork. We were so happy to see the Nazis arrested so quickly. The Dutch had the names and addresses of all the Germans. The minute the German invasion began, they were arrested. There were lots of Nazis in Java. The man, whose wife I was a companion for, was arrested. The German prisoners were put on two boats to be sent to India. One of the boats hit a mine in the harbor. It sank and all those bastards were drowned. The other boat reached India.

There were two Jews who did clandestine business with Japan. The Dutch Army was looking for them. They were caught in the hills trying to escape and were put in prison until the boats were loaded for India. They were on the boat that sank.

Japan Takes Java

I remember December 7, 1941. The head doctor came in and told me about the surprise attack on Pearl Harbor, and that the war had begun. We had expected it, because the Japanese Navy had been patrolling off the coast of Luzon, in the Philippines, since the invasion of Holland in May 1940. There was no resistance to the Japanese invasion of Java.

Don't let anybody tell you differently. The Japs came to Singapore, then to Sumatra and then to Java. They wanted the oil and rubber for their war machine, and there was plenty around. I knew of two refineries; the Palembong in Sumatra and the Belenba, which was a big Royal Dutch Shell Oil refinery in Borneo. The Dutch were colonialists, who over the centuries, treated the Indonesians as second class citizens. They kept them illiterate and in poverty. Many of the native people deeply resented the Dutch and the English.

After the attack on Pearl Harbor, the Japanese invaded the Dutch Indies on March 1, 1942. Some of the soldiers came on bicycles to Batavia, which is now known as Jakarta. The country was on a war footing. The head Dutch doctor called me in and told me that I was now in the Dutch Army. He asked, "Do you want to escape? That's treason." I asked, "Escape to where?" I knew Australia was not far away, but they didn't want us. Australia played a very bad role. They said no; we don't want the so called white people from Indonesia. So I knew there was no use in going there. The sea from Java was very rough, and those old freighters would never make it. Some people may have tried to escape, but I know they didn't make it to Australia. I served four years and nine months in the Dutch Army.

Life in Java before the Japs invaded was good. I loved my job in the children's ward of the hospital. I had good friends and my dog, Fifi. He died of rabies a few months before the war started. There were no shots to cure him. He jumped out the window. We never saw him again. Lots of people looked for him. It was hopeless.

Japan Opened Prison Camps

Shortly after the Japanese occupied Java, they began to set

up prison camps. I didn't get arrested until October 1, 1943. Upon the invasion, the Dutch men were immediately arrested. Mr. Jacobson was arrested and died in prison two years later. I never saw the Dutch doctor from my hospital until after the war.

Before I was arrested, I remember I had to take my nurse's exam. Two Indonesian doctors gave the exams in Pandu Bahasas, the Indonesian language. I knew enough of the language to get by and passed the exam. The Indonesian doctors took over the hospital and ran it with a Christian nurse, who was ten years older than I.

In October 1943, the Japanese came in a car to pick us up and take us to an office. One said, "We want that white woman." I was told I could take one suitcase. The Japanese decided to round up all German Jews. They had left us alone for awhile. Nietje, an Indonesian woman, who had become one of my best friends had warned me that the Japs would be coming to arrest me. She offered to hide me at her home in her village. I said, "No. It will be too dangerous for you. If they catch you, they will kill you and your family. Besides, I am a white woman and it would be impossible to hide me in your village."

I arrived at a prison in Cheribon which was located on the coast of Java. The prison was for women only. The men were put in a different camp nearby. The women prisoners in my camp included a Dutch doctor's wife, with two kids, a German woman in her fifties, a Danish woman, whose husband was a businessman in Java and her daughter, who was a little younger than I was. Another prisoner was the wife of a Jewish dentist, whose office was in Cheribon. We remained in that prison camp for six months.

Life was very hard there. They brought something for

breakfast that no one could eat. We all had mosquito nets. Flies! Oh, God! Mosquitoes! They were even worse than the flies. It started raining in December, and when it rains it pours. The sewer ran over every night. The Japanese guards came in and said, "Here's a broom, you sweep it out." The Danish girl and I cleaned the sewers every night. Her name was Karin. Some of the guards opened the metal door. They told us to get water from the spigot in the bath house. We needed many pails of water. We got eczema on our feet and legs. It was terrible. We didn't have shoes or rubber boots – just our bare feet. That happened a few more times during the rainy season. Karin didn't get sick. They separated us when we were sent to different prison camps.

We were locked up in a cell from six at night until six in the morning. When they opened the cells, we could go to the big washroom. In order to clean the cells, we had to carry some water from the washroom. I got big muscles. We got jungle rot on our feet. It never did heal.

Once a month, each of us was interviewed by the Campeytie, their Gestapo. They asked foolish questions. The Dutch woman, with her two children, was in a cell next to mine. I would knock on her wall, but couldn't make contact with her. Her poor husband had been killed by the Japanese. He was in charge of the oil drilling in Java. I had met him once. They asked me in the interview if I knew him. I said, "No, I don't know anything about him." That's why I said, don't ask foolish questions. It must have been very hard on her to hear the men screaming in the prison next to ours. We heard all kinds of terrible beatings. One of the men was a guy I knew when I stayed at their home in Bandung, before I began working in the hospital. He was head of the train services in Java. They finally killed him. I saw the killing through a hole in the big metal door that we could look through. I wish I hadn't witnessed it. One day I saw the Jewish dentist and he was fine. The next day, they had broken his arm. It was very bad.

Every morning the head of the prison camp came into our cell block for inspection. We had to strip our beds and clean the washrooms. One day this German woman didn't want to get up. I said, "You'd better get up when the Japs come in. You've got to bow deeply." She wouldn't. They were just about ready to beat her up in front of me. This Jewish woman was about fifty years old. I went very politely to the Japanese guards and asked if I could talk with them. I told the guards that this woman was a little crazy, but I was going to teach her to behave and to please let me teach her some manners. The two Japs talked a little while, and one said, "Okay, you teach her." And they let me. So there was no beating up on her. Oh God! But one day this Danish girl threw a banana to the native gardener on the outside of the prison. Boy, did she get a beating. Terrible! I told her, "You have to obey them. You don't do things in here that make the Japs angry."

After six months, we were moved by train from Cheribon to a new prison in Jakarta. It had been a large house. The houses were probably owned by very rich white people. They put barbed wire around the prison to keep us from trying to escape. Even if we could escape, they would catch us immediately because we were white. They said our eyes were of the enemy. We heard that many times. They'd say, "You are white. You better get the hell out of here." They put us with some other prisoners who were already there. I don't even know where they came from, but they were very nice people. I worked in the prison hospital, so I got to eat good food. The native women fed us well. Some of the people were sick. For the first time, I saw someone who had twelve day fever, which is a tropical typhus. He was in isolation. Before I was arrested, I had seen a patient with bubonic plague. I worried because of the fleas on the rats that bite people. That could happen to us. We could contract the plague.

I was in that camp for six months. It got stricter and stricter. We could get out of our cells to go to the court-yard in the daytime. If you had to go to the bathroom in the middle of the night, you would climb over a wall and down a ladder. The bathroom facilities were horrible. A woman and a little girl shared my room. Her husband was in another camp nearby. One day he came to tell us France was finally invaded by the Allies. That was on June 6, 1944, which was called D-Day.

The head of all the Japanese camps had his headquarters on the street outside the prison. One day he called me in to talk. He was very nice to me and said, "You know, you look like my daughter." I felt very flattered. I bowed deeply, many times; that's what you do when you greet them. He said he missed his family in Japan.

In September, we heard there was an invasion of Africa by the Allies. Our hopes arose. We thought we would be liberated soon. But shortly after that, we had to pack up, were put on a train and taken to the Tangerang prison. We were marched to the camp where everything changed for the worst. It was a very bad prison. The bunks were like wooden tables, but not separate bunks. We had very little to eat. I remember the rats. Rats! Oh, God! I didn't have kids, so I slept on the top bunk, and the poor woman with kids had to sleep on the bottom with the rats, big ones. I had to kill the rats with a big stick. The toilets were open in a big shower room. In the beginning of October, everyone got sick with malaria and jaundice. I was as yellow as you can imagine. Everybody threw up. I didn't have it as badly as the others. One day, I couldn't get up. I was doing poorly. To go down to the bathroom, you had to climb down a ladder. When I got better, I got very hungry. It was terrible. Less than fifteen of the prisoners lived. I don't even know what the main meal was. I know there was no breakfast. Period! They told me to get a kind of tapioca that pumped up my stomach. I ate it and threw up.

The guards counted us every day. I had to go to open all the cells and see how the people were doing. One day, some rice and sugar arrived by truck. We had to unload it. I carried one hundred pound sacks on my back. I didn't have to, but I felt very bad. I couldn't let the sick people do it. It was not right. So I carried all of the sacks. Some girls, who worked in the so-called office, came by and asked me to help them. They said, "We must have quinine to fight this malaria." The Japs had a quinine factory nearby. When this Japanese guy called me to his office, I bowed to him again. I said, "Excuse me, can we have quinine? The mosquitoes are biting us, and they will bite you, oh, yes!" He sat there in silence. I said many thanks and left. The next day we had quinine. I had scared them, but it is true; mosquitoes don't care who they bite. To handle the problems of malaria, the Japanese had a powder that burns, and the smell gets rid of the mosquitoes. They began to burn it in our cell block. The quinine was in big pills and was really nasty. I took one and I didn't care if it was not easy to swallow. I took them. I told the other prisoners they must take the pills. If you don't, malaria can kill us because we're already so weak. They agreed.

There were Jews from Singapore and Malaysia in our camp. I practiced my English with them. In this camp, the prisoners were mostly Dutch people from Java, Borneo and Sumatra. Winter had arrived, and they moved us again to another camp in Jakarta. The prisoners were not separated this time. This prison camp was something else! We heard rumors about the invasion of the Philippines. We were not allowed to have newspapers. No news! Nothing! We learned about the outside world from rumors. Radios were not allowed. As the prisoners came and went, they told us about the invasion of the Philippines and Manila. They told us about the Allies landing on the Marshall Islands. It was an island hopping war, as you called it. We wanted to know, why don't they liberate us? When we arrived at the new prison, we walked in a caravan. It was very difficult because we were very weak. We walked straight up a hill. We arrived in Adeck in the afternoon. The Japs told us our suitcases would be unloaded in the morning. We were given cornbread. I hadn't eaten so much bread in all my life. On that first night, I could not sleep because I had no pillow, no blanket and no mosquito net. I just walked around and didn't sleep. By this time we had the constant runs. The next morning our suitcases arrived, and we carried them to our rooms. I got my junk, and junk it was!

The following day, the younger girls from Singapore told me we had bad trouble. The cesspool was full, and they were ordered to clean it. I said I would see what I could do. Again, we were counted in the morning and at night. When the guards came, this time the head of all camps, including Thijdang, the big one, came over and asked if I needed anything. I pointed to the cesspool. I said, "We'll get dysentery and typhus. If we get typhus, everybody gets typhus. Oh, yes! Everybody gets it!" The next morning, before I awoke, the workmen had already come and cleaned the cesspool. I was so proud!

I never saw that Japanese commandant again. In that camp, I saw the white people who had been tortured. The favorite torture was to pull out fingernails. They would take cigarette butts and burn the skin. Even the women and children did not escape that torture. I knew a woman they called Ochi, which means old one. She really wasn't so old, but being locked up made her look old. The guards stood at the door, kicked it in, caught her and beat her. For what, I don't know. They gave one girl the water treatment, by pouring an enema bag of water on her face. They poured water on her face, to force it into her stomach, to make her think she was drowning. Then they beat her. Today, when I hear about water boarding, I get furious; absolutely furious!

One of the young Japs took the girls from Singapore and Malaysia, who were much younger than I, and abused them. One Jap, who loved Hitler, came over to me and asked, "Whose rug is this?" I didn't argue with him, I just cleaned it. When he left, I told the girls we have to be liberated! Until then, we have to keep up our spirits.

Toward the end of May, another group of prisoners arrived. They were native women from central Java who told me the war in Europe was over. Germany had surrendered. I said, "What?" They said, "Don't make a fuss." I said, "No, I won't. Peace will come. We will be rescued."

We got less and less to eat. Then a food relief agency dropped packages from a plane onto the prison yard. Because they were so clumsy, the big packages fell on, and killed some prisoners. It was very bad. I didn't want to eat any of that stuff, but I had to. The packages contained tobacco, soap, dried milk, sugar and instant coffee. I exchanged the tobacco for soap, and the milk for toothpaste. That was the first toothpaste we had seen in years. Most of the women and children had very bad teeth. When the cavities hurt, I would put little red or green peppers into the hole. You leave it in until it burns a nerve. That's what we had to do in the camp to take away the pain. The children cried and cried.

In June, we got another package with some cooked eggs. We mixed the eggs with a little rice. The women were going to throw away the egg shells. I said, "No! We're going to use them to clean our teeth. You scrape your teeth with them. And then we'll crush the shells and eat them for the calcium. Nothing is to be thrown away. Except, you never eat a banana peel, because it's poisonous."

As the days passed, our guards got angrier and angrier with us. This camp held eleven hundred Dutch people and eleven hundred non-Dutch. I asked for two aides each to work in the Dutch and Jewish blocks. Many of the prisoners had fleas and lice, so you had to be very careful. I rolled my hair up in a bun to keep them out.

We began to meet and talk with each other in the camp. The guards got mad, really mad! One day they demanded that every prisoner go out into the field. They counted us. It was 8 a.m., and by then Java gets very hot. We stood in the field for four hours in the boiling sun. One woman couldn't stand any more. She sat down and they beat the hell out of her. That woman was almost 65. It was a terrible day.

Toward the end of July, we still knew very little about the war. We were not liberated until August 30, 1945. There was a big noise in the Japanese barracks. On the other side of the wall, they were screaming like mad in Japanese. We didn't know what was happening. I asked a girl, who had been an interpreter for her father, who was a businessman in Japan, to interpret. She said that Japan had been bombed very badly, and they were screaming, "The war is over!" Of course, this good news spread like wildfire. We all went out into the field. I told everybody to be quiet; that we had to obey them, because no one had rescued us yet.

The next day, one woman didn't want to go to the work detail and told the Japs off. She said, "Sweep your own floor." They dragged her into the cage in the hot sun and kept her there for 48 hours with no water, no toilet, no nothing. She ranted and raved. She survived. I don't know how.

I gave pep talks to keep up the spirits of my fellow prisoners. We were told, on the 15th of August, that we would get more to eat and lots of rice did arrive. I told everybody to wait; if we get more to eat, then we'll know the war is over. On the 15th of August, Sukarno arrived in Jakarta to declare independence. The Japs had shipped him in to take over the country after they left. We got a little more water and a little more food to eat every day. It was good they didn't give us too much right away, because that would have made us sick. On August 30, 1945, Queen Wilhelmina's birthday, we were assembled in the prison yard. The big Belgian woman, the quisling, shouted, "The war is not over yet. You aren't going anywhere." In defiance, we stood and sang the Dutch national anthem.

HET KONINKLIJL HUIS

Tekst van het Wilhemus

Wilhemus van Nassouwe
Ben ick van Duytschen Bloedt

Den Vanderland ghetrouwe
Blijf ick tot inden doet;
Een Prince van Grangien
Ben ick vry onverveert
Den Coninck van Hispangien
Heb ick aitijt gheeert.

In Godes vrees te eleven
Heb ick altijt betracht,
Daerom be ick verdreven
Om Land, om Luyd ghebracht:
Maer Godt sal my regeren
Al seen goet Instrument,
Dat ick sat wederkeeren
In mijen Regiment.
Lijdt U, mijn Ondersaten,
Die oprecht zijn van aert,
Godt sal u niet veriaten
Al zijt ghy nu beswaert:
Die vroom begheert te leven,
Bidt Godt nacht ended ach.
Dat Hy my cracht wil gheven
Dat ick u helpen mach.

Lijf ende goed al te semen
Heb ick u niet verschoont,
Mijn Broeders, hooch van Namen,
Hebbent u oock vertoont;
Graef Adolff is Ghebieven,
In Vrieslandt in den Slach,
Sijn siel int eewich leven
Verwacht den jonghsten dach.

Edel en Hooch gheboren
Van Keyserlicken stam:
Een Vorst des Rijks vercoren,
Al seen vroom Christen-man,
Voor Godes Woort ghepreesen,
Heb ick vrij onversaecht,
Al seen helt zonder vreesen
Mijn endel bloet gewaecht.
Mijn schilt ende betrouwen

The Belgian woman turned pale and hurriedly ran out. We knew the war was over. At last, we were free. Pretty soon the Dutch men from the nearby prison camps came to get their women and children. They were united again and very happy. Of course, because I was alone, I didn't have anybody to come to get me. So, I went to the office and asked "What do you want me to do?" I was told to go to work at the Saint Carolus Catholic Hospital.

I knew I had been saved when they dropped the atomic bomb on Hiroshima. Prisoners were dying everyday. We would not have lasted much longer. I had contracted beri-beri (caused by a lack of Vitamin B1 and thiamine in the diet) and was very weak. I had lost so much weight that I was skin and bones. The jaundice left brown marks on me. Our bellies were extended from malnourishment. I was asked to use a syringe to remove the fluid from the swollen body of one of the prisoners. We were filled with pain and hopelessness. If the bomb had not been dropped, we would have died. Today I am against nuclear war. I am against using nuclear fuel because there is no safe way of disposing of the remnants. I don't know if bombing Nagasaki was necessary. I doubt it.

I never went back to the camp. Oh, no! Before I left that afternoon, I threw my mattress, pillow, bedding and stuff onto an open patch in the prison field. I put my tattered belongings down, got some paper, soaked it with petrol and set it on fire. Those fleas, bed bugs and lice burned up. As I watched it burn, I smiled with relief.

Heinrich Jacobson, 1940, a Dutch executive with the
Palmolive Company in Java. Lilo is standing next
to her benefactor.

Lilo in Java, 1939. Nora Jacobson's mother gave
this bicycle to Lilo.

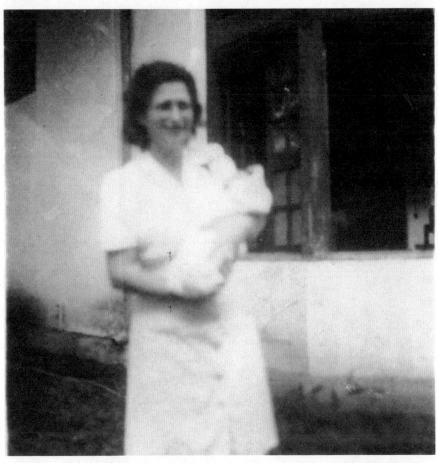

Lilo, 1940, with an infant she delivered as a mid-wife at
the Dutch Hospital in Java.

Lilo, 1941, with her dog, Fifi.

Lilo, 1945, after her imprisonment by the Japanese.

CHAPTER IV

Civil War in the Dutch East Indies

At the conclusion of World War II, I began my nursing duties at the Saint Carolus Hospital in Jakarta. When the staff from the hospital drove me from the prison camp to the hospital, they said they would find me a decent room in the nurses building. That night we heard lots of shooting. That was the beginning of the Civil War between the Indonesians and the Dutch. My roommate was a nice Dutch girl. I don't know what she did during the war. You never asked many questions. We stayed at that hospital until Easter of the next year.

My first patients were 70 men and women who came from the prison camps and were suffering from serious malnutrition. Most of them recovered, except for one kid from the Middle East. One night, I sat with him until he died. I don't know if he heard me tell him that the war was over and that we had to fight to live. But, I knew he was dead because he had turned blue.

Other patients had malaria. Some of the women had just

dclivered. If their babies didn't get antibiotics, they would die. We had to be careful because the medicine was strong and it could kill the babies if we didn't give them the right dosage. The native women from Kampong, a nearby village, worked in the hospital. They cooked the meals, washed the dishes at night and cleaned the floors and the windows. They worked every day for very little pay and no appreciation for their hard work. I developed very good relations with them. When I worked the afternoon shift, before I went to bed, I generally checked on everything and helped the workers finish their chores.

The nuns were from Holland. They wore blue habits with white starched wimples. I didn't know much about Catholics but these nuns were very strict. A few were mixed. They worked hard and prayed a lot. One of the young nuns had grey blue eyes and very white skin. She saw this cute priest who was leading prayers early one morning. She told me she wanted to go see him. I said, "Go ahead." I don't know what her relationship with the priest was. I didn't ask. I didn't want to know. I grew up knowing very little about Catholicism. There was only one Catholic school and a church in Liegnitz.

The Native Women Walk Out

One morning, the nun, who ran the hospital, called me. She was alarmed because none of the native women had shown up for work. The nuns had made a rule that forbid the women from taking any leftover food with them back to the village. I asked what they did with the leftover food. They said they threw it away. These people were hungry and their children needed the food. In my eye, to this day, that is a sin. It's terrible! Every night, the nuns would frisk the women to see if they had any food or medicine on them. The women resented this. They felt humiliated. I told the nuns that I would go to the village to ask them to return to work. But first, I asked the nuns, "Are you going to give them the food? Are you going to continue to search them every night? Are you going to continue to mistreat them?" They promised they would not do those bad things anymore, if only they would come back to work. The women's anger toward the Dutch was growing.

When the nuns told the Dutch officers that I was going to the village to try to get the hospital help to return to work, they said I would be shot if I did such a foolish thing. I told them nobody is going to kill me. So, I went to the native village with the Dutch soldiers tagging along. I told them to wait outside the village. I would go in alone, because I did not want to frighten the women and children with soldiers by my side carrying guns.

The houses were made of woven straw. You had to walk up a set of steps to enter the houses. They were built on stilts. Chickens ran around underneath their houses. The mattresses they slept on were filled with a fluffy fruit from the local trees. It looked like feathers, but it wasn't.

When I walked into the village, the women came running out and invited me to see where they lived. "Please come to my hut," they said. I had some food and bandages. I had to climb up a short ladder to get into a hut. I put bandages on the children's sores and gave them some food. We laughed and talked. Finally, I said, "I'd better get back to work." I asked them if they would return to work at the hospital. "You want me to come back?" one asked. We continued to talk until they said they were ready to come back with me. So, about 30 of them walked with me as we left the village on our way back to the hospital. You should have seen the faces of the soldiers, who thought they were there to rescue me. We settled the problem peacefully. I told the women that the nuns had promised to give them medicine, bandages and leftover food. Most of the children had malaria. So they all got medicine from then on. They were allowed to take the leftover food back to their families. The women never missed work again. The nuns changed their bad ways. They no longer frisked the women. They never threw any food away again.

One morning, the nuns told me that the soldiers were coming to check for weapons; that they would search the women. I objected and told them that no weapons were hidden on my ward. If they did search the women, I told the soldiers I would be with them to speak their native language, and to assure them they had nothing to fear. Sure enough, the big gate opened and the soldiers came in. Once more, I told the soldiers that these are babies and sick women, so be very careful. Of course, they didn't find any weapons. The soldiers apologized and left.

The Civil War Grows

I was caught in the Civil War between the Dutch and the Indonesians. A girl, with whom I shared the mosquito net in prison, was riding a bicycle with her mother and sister in the hills above the hospital when the natives came, ripped off the bicycles and threw them in the channel. She was drowned.

The Dutch weren't going to stay in Indonesia. The transition was very difficult. One day I saw a little fruit stand down the street from the hospital. I went to buy a banana.

Suddenly an older man warned me, "You run back to the hospital. You are going to get killed." I went back as fast as I could, leaving my banana behind. Suddenly I heard a boom. I hadn't gone very far, because I was too weak. I heard the shooting. Bullets were flying past my head.

Things settled down for a little while in Jakarta. One afternoon I went downtown to shop at the little Chinese stores. On the way back to my house it became dark. In Java, which is near the equator, night comes very quickly – just a matter of a few minutes between daylight and darkness. It's that sudden. There I was in pitch darkness, in the middle of a civil war. Boy, I was scared. As I ran, I could hear gunfire. An open Dutch Army truck came rolling by and stopped. I climbed into the back, where everyone was hiding. Before I got home, the shooting had begun. That was the beginning of November 1945. I didn't go out again until March 1946. Shooting, shooting, shooting. One of the Dutch doctors said he was taking the train to visit friends in another part of Java. I begged him to stay at the hospital. He went anyway. We learned that when the train stopped at his station, a gang of rebels ambushed him. They cut him into pieces with big knives and left him to die on the station platform.

On another occasion, a Dutch Christian nurse told me she was going to attend mass on Sunday. I begged her to stay. "Don't take any chances," I said. She went anyway. While they were attending mass, the rebels came and built fires and burned the church to the ground. She was killed in the fire. Our fears grew more with each passing day. What would they do next? We knew it would be bad! They said, "This is our country. You get out!" Some of the people were very angry with the Dutch.

Those with mixed blood, Dutch and Indonesian, were

singled out by the insurgents. About thirty mixed people lived in a small village near our hospital. I knew they would be killed if we did not do something. I urged the nuns at the hospital to take them in for their protection. We kept them for several weeks until things settled down. The civil war was ripping the country apart. No one was safe.

My Mother Finds Me

I knew my poor parents wanted to know what had happened to their only daughter. They were living in Ecuador. Some British soldiers had come from Burma through Singapore. They told me horrible stories. They had to go through the jungle, where they slept under trees and could hear Japanese airplanes flying over them. The war ended for them in Mandalay. I told the British army soldiers that I wanted to find my parents. The only thing I remembered was a post office box in Quito, Ecuador. They couldn't help me.

Finally, I heard from my parents. I had not seen them for eight years, since we parted in 1939. A Jewish girlfriend, who had escaped to London from Nazi Germany in 1939, contacted the International Red Cross. She told the officials that I had escaped to Java in 1939. She gave them my address at Tjideres Hospital in Jakarta, where I worked before the war. The Red Cross checked with all the hospitals until they finally found me. The Red Cross located me and sent a notice to my mother saying that I was alive, had been a prisoner of war and was currently working at the Saint Carolus Hospital in Batavia.

In her first letter in years, my mother wrote telling me how happy they were to learn that I was alive. She said my father suffered a stroke and was paralyzed. My mother was working in the library in Quito, the capital of Ecuador. My father had started a business when they first located there. His company made cement pipes. The business was going very well until he had a stroke. Then he couldn't work any more.

Most of our family and friends, who had remained in Nazi Germany, died in concentration camps. My mother had developed diabetes, which then interfered with my parents' chances to come to the United States. Immigrants who were sick were not allowed entry. We had friends in San Francisco. She must have moved heaven and earth to help me. I told my parents that I had to get out of Java. I feared for my life. The Civil War was becoming more dangerous every day. My mother was a very capable woman. Although she didn't speak a word of English, she spoke fluent Spanish and French. She had completed thirteen years of study in Germany. My mother wrote to my Uncle Martin, my father's brother in Pennsylvania, about my grave situation. He was an engineer for a car construction company. I told my mother I wanted to go to San Francisco. Finally, he got his act together, got me an affidavit and sent money for my trip to America. My affidavit came in a diplomatic pouch. Getting out of Java was not easy.

Someone came from the American Embassy and said they wanted to see me the next afternoon. So the next day, I went to the American Embassy. I saw a very nice young man, Mr. Wolf, who said we have an affidavit here. It came through the diplomatic pouch with all those official letters. He said your mother is working to have a boat stop in Jakarta and then go to San Francisco. He said I would need an exit visa.

They neglected to say I needed shots before entering the

United States. Before the war, before I was arrested, I did get a combination of typhus, cholera and dysentery shots each year. But from 1943 to 1946, I didn't get shots because I was in several prison camps, where the Japanese refused to give us shots. I came to Manila and they would not let me off the boat.

The Dutch made trouble for me. I made an appointment to get an exit visa. When I came to the office, they said they were too busy. I had to come back three times. I will never forget that, but I did forgive them. Finally, at the last minute, I got the visa. They told me that a boat from Bombay, a freighter, would stop in Jakarta and then go on to San Francisco by way of Manila.

I had a few things to do before the boat came. I stopped working at the hospital. I still had the nurses uniform, but I wanted civilian clothes. I asked if there was someone who could make me a dress. I said, "I will pay for it." Finally a woman said she would make the dress. You've got to fight for things. I had to fight every day just to survive.

We were scheduled to leave Jakarta on July 5th so I took my junk and went to the harbor. They said the boat was not leaving until tomorrow at 4 o'clock. It was too dangerous to stay at the dock, so I took a rickshaw back to Jakarta. I didn't want to go back to the hospital, so I went to some friends I knew and asked if I could sleep overnight. They gave me a bed and a mosquito net. My blood was very thin with very little hemoglobin. You still get bitten and, with one bite, you get malaria. You better not scratch. For every scratch you get an infection. I stayed there overnight and the next morning they gave me coffee and cornbread. One asked, "Why don't you come with us to Singapore?" I said, "I am not going there. I am going to San Francisco." I returned to the boat at 4 pm and we left Jakarta.

The first stop was at a dirty little village, without even a paved street from the harbor to downtown. I saw only warehouses. Anyway, that was my trip. The freighter carried about ten passengers. The boat was shot at by members of the Indonesian Freedom Movement, as we passed a small island.

We stopped to load copra, a dried coconut meat. I remember being afraid that night while they loaded the freighter at Makassar. We passed a huge Shell Oil refinery. Suddenly the captain appeared and said, "Nobody move! Stay where you are and be very still! We are in dangerous waters. There are mines out there." I saw one mine, a ball with a string on top. It bobbled on the waves as we passed it. We got through safely and from there on it was just more ocean until we arrived in Manila.

Upon arrival we could not go inside the breakwater. The first thing the harbor patrolman asked was, "Do you have all your shots and where are the papers? Shots are necessary if you want to go to the United States." By the way, I was the only refugee on the freighter, so I got my shots right away. A week later I had to come back to the freighter for another shot.

I met a young rabbi in Manila, who had been a friend of my family in Germany. I went to his house. They had fled the house the night the Japanese burned the harbor. Manila was destroyed during the war. The post office was just a shell of a building. Standing in it you could see the sky. I mailed my parents a postcard from Manila.

Finally, in July 1946, I sailed to America. I was only 25 years old, but had already had some unbelievable stories to tell. Telling them would wait a while. I was unable to tell these stories for many years. The pain inside me shut my past out.

Indonesia, formally The Dutch East Indies, became a
Republic in 1949.

George Basch, early 1940's, in Quito, Ecuador, with a
worker at his cement pipe company.

Johanna and George Basch in Quito, Ecuador. George
had suffered a stroke and died before seeing Lilo again.

1 CM.267.575   61

COMITÉ INTERNATIONAL DE LA CROIX-ROUGE

GENÈVE (Suisse)

DEMANDEUR — ANFRAGESTELLER — ENQUIRER

Nom - *Name* WEISSENBERG .

Prénom - *Vorname* - *Christian name* Dorothea .

Rue - *Strasse* - *Street* 2 Wadham Place .

Localité - *Ortschaft* - *Locality* Holywell St .

Département - *Provinz* - *County* OXFORD .

Pays - *Land* - *Country* England

Message à transmettre — Mitteilung — Message

(25 mots au maximum, nouvelles de caractère strictement personnel et
familial) — (nicht über 25 Worte, nur persönliche Familiennachrichten) —
(not over 25 words, family news of strictly personal character).

Dear Bully. We are very glad with
letter. Without message of Fredy since
august 1944. Erni, Inge, Ilmo send
regards and best wishes.
                Cordially. Thea.

Date - *Datum* 9 - 10 . 45 .

DESTINATAIRE — EMPFÄNGER — ADDRESSEE

Nom - *Name* BASCH .

Prénom - *Vorname* - *Christian name* nurse Lilo . P.O.W.

Rue - *Strasse* - *Street* C.R.I 65-88 .

Localité - *Ortschaft* - *Locality* St. Carolus Red Cross Hospital

Province - *Provinz* - *County* BATAVIA - SALEMBA

Pays - *Land* - *Country* JAVA . (N. India)

RÉPONSE AU VERSO   ANTWORT UMSEITUNG   REPLY OVERLEAF
Prière d'écrire très lisiblement Bitte sehr deutlich schreiben Please write very clearly

The International Red Cross 1945 inquiry

64

CHAPTER V

My Return to East Germany in 1984

❧

I went back to East Germany, not West Germany, in 1984. In San Francisco, I belonged to an organization, a friendship society, that worked to encourage peace in this country as well as in Eastern Europe, mainly East Germany. The woman in charge of the society said, "We want you to go to East Germany, as a delegate to an international peace conference. You pay for your flight but everything in the country will be paid by the East Germans." Some of the other delegates were teachers from Oakland and American Communist Party members. I was not a member of the Communist Party, but I was chosen as a delegate and agreed to go. We took a night flight to Frankfurt. I had been in Frankfurt in the summer of 1938, when the airport had just opened. That was where the Germans flew the Zeppelin. Frankfurt didn't look like it did in 1938. There were lots of destruction and lots of rebuilding. We changed planes for our flight to Berlin. We landed at a small airport, not the main airport at Tempelholf. We had to wait at the airport for the people from East Germany to meet us. I remember seeing the Berlin Wall as we drove to the Eastern Sector.

We had to wait quite a while to be allowed to go through West Berlin. We were taken to The Hotel Berlin, where we had dinner. The next day was May Day. We marched in the big parade, walking arm in arm with women from many countries who were dedicated to having peace in the world. We walked through the streets of East Berlin to Karl Marx Platz.

When I returned to the hotel, I called a woman in Berlin who had visited her mother in Berkeley, California the year before. Her mother had died since then and a friend of hers gave me letters and things to give her daughter. That wasn't too difficult. That night I said, "I have to call my husband." They said that call would cost forty-two marks. I said, "All right. I have to call my husband!" The telephone was old fashioned. The operator connected me to the hotel in Alexander Platz. Everybody was excited, especially the telephone girl who made the call. My husband was excited to hear from me. I am sure that the Stazis, the secret police in East Germany, were listening in. I didn't care.

At the peace conference, they talked with us about the German Democratic Republic. We were given papers to read. English was spoken but the papers, of course, were in German, so I had lots to read. I traveled with other delegates from the peace conference. The next day we visited a concentration camp, which was very upsetting. On the following day we visited Potsdam. As a kid, I always wanted to go there. My parents raved about it. We visited the main castle and saw the beautiful paintings.

A visitor gave me a calendar of all the buildings that Frederick the Great had built. Luckily, the Russians did not burn or bomb Potsdam. The beautiful gardens were left intact. I saw the street where the Huguenots lived when they came to Germany, in the seventeenth century. We drove around Potsdam and held a meeting at the very place where President Truman, Premier Stalin and Prime Minister Churchill met in 1945 to divide Europe. We had a beautiful lunch. It was the first time in my life I saw white asparagus.

I was asked if there was any place I wanted to go to talk with the East German people. I said, "I want to visit a school." When I arrived at the school, I noticed there were no computers, but they had old adding machines and calculators. The kids were playing ball out in the yard and everything looked so nice.

A Divided Germany

Mistakes were made in Potsdam. Stalin insisted on a certain border to divide Germany, which was completely incorrect. When you chase people out of their land, you chase their history out as well. Stalin insisted that Breslau be Polish, as well as my hometown of Liegnitz. Stalin gave our mountains in Silesia to Poland. What did mountains have to do with politics? To this day, I remember every trail I went on. Those memories cannot be eradicated. I feel that Berlin should never have been divided. You cannot divide a city like that. It is ridiculous! You cannot make it an International City. You have to unite the country. The way it was divided was wrong.

The younger people in East Berlin were leaving in droves. The only people left in some of the small towns were older Germans. That was a problem. That's what you get when you destroy a whole people – a whole country. In the region I grew up in, Silesia, you had to now speak Polish and not German. I was in East Germany for three weeks.

As I traveled from checkpoint to checkpoint, as an official visitor, I talked with many people; farmers, workers and simple family people. I met a newspaper person, Margaret, who was born in Germany. She wrote articles about unification. I was able to travel by train to my mother's birthplace, Rostock, on the Baltic. I saw some of the most beautiful apartment houses. Rostock has a very rough climate, lots of wind and icy weather. I went to the beach to see the beautiful sand I had loved to walk on as a youngster. I wanted to get my feet wet. It was so cold. I took the train back to the main street, which was called the Long Street.

Rostock Was Different

In Rostock, I walked down the main street past the university. I vaguely remember being there as a four year old child. I remembered that the main building was a department store. Today, it's a headquarters of the Farmers' Party. I walked out into a little park and sat down on a bench and looked around. I remember sitting there with my nursemaid in 1925. I remembered the wall and the buildings. Anyway, that was some experience. I only wish my mother could have been with me on that day to see her hometown.

One morning I went to a delicatessen to buy some bread and sausage. I also asked for smoked eel and ate it. I bought some stuff to take back to the railway station. As I walked, I saw where my grandparents had lived. I kept that image all those years in my mind. One day I went into the village to a café. I sat down. That is the only bad experience I had in Rostock. I sat down and no one would wait on me. Nobody would wait on me! I got up to ask the manager. I said, "Don't you serve lunch?" I didn't even get an answer. He looked at me angrily. I walked out. It was not good to be back in Germany. As a country, it was so strange. I never want to go back.

On the train ride back to Berlin, I met some German farmers and shared stories with them. One man worked in the fields and his wife prepared vegetables for canning. They said they were both very happy. "We have work. We have food. We have a son in the East German Army. He was drafted for two years. He will come back and we will see what he does with his life."

When I returned to Berlin, the peace conference director asked me if I would like to go to a museum. I said, "No, I didn't want to go to that museum because in November 1938, when my father and I were in Berlin, we were not allowed to enter that museum." I had a choice of going to the museum or meeting with some East German people from the peace organization. I said I wanted to talk with the people. I went with the group to get coffee and cakes. The coffee was excellent, but I am not much for cakes. I ate a little to be polite. You eat what is in front of you. On one trip we saw the statue where the Soviet soldier is holding a German child. We went to a co-operative and talked with a person who had been in prison under Hitler. Another one said he had spent the war in Shanghai, where he learned how to fix cars. They were Jews who survived. A number of Jews lived out the war years in China, especially Shanghai. On one of our trips, the group took me to a factory where they made children's clothing. I had worked as a bookkeeper in a factory that made boy's jeans when I first came to San Francisco. The factory looked very advanced and clean. We were shown the houses where they lived and a state farm, a co-operative. I liked being on the farm because it reminded me of growing up in Liegnitz; but Liegnitz was gone now! All the archives were burned by the Poles. Everyone speaks Polish. No other member of my family was alive in Germany. The town didn't exist for me anymore. That made me very sad. The last night, we stayed in a hotel in Alexander Platz. On that last day it was raining, but I did walk to Alexander Platz and bought a book about Rostock. The East German Peace Committee had a party to see us off. We left the next day for our homelands. I knew I would never return. There was no reason to. My hometown was gone. A favorite uncle was killed in Bergen - Belsen. His wife and their son did escape to Australia. There are all those terrible memories of the Nazis.

When most people return to their hometown, their family and friends welcome them with love. They talk about old times. I had not seen Liegnitz for forty-five years. On my return, there was no one to greet me. I felt a terrible void. All my family that had remained, even the young ones, had been killed by the Nazis. I felt completely alone. No, I will never go back.